# Contents

# Portraits

This is a photograph of Britain's royal family.

This family asked the artist to paint a picture of them. There were no cameras when this was painted.

*The Capel Family* by Cornelius Johnson (c. 1640)

# Mummy

This mummy and child is carved out of stone.

*Maternity* by Henry Moore (1924)

# Can you see the marks made by the coloured chalk?

# Daddy

This daddy is with his daughter in their garden.

What colours has the artist used to paint this picture?

Eugene Manet with his Daughter at Bougival by Berthe Morisot (c. 1881)

9

# Sister

This little girl has been painted with her baby sister. What is she holding in her hand?

Li'l Sis by William H Johnson (1944)

Look at the light and dark
parts of this painting.

# Brother

Don Manuel Osorio de Zuniga by Francisco Jose de Goya Y Lucientes (c. 1788–89)

This little boy was a prince.

12

Do you have a brother?
Does he wear clothes like this?

# What are these two brothers doing?

13

# Grandma

This painting is of a girl with her mummy and grandma.

# Look at the light and dark parts of this painting.

15

# Grandad

Grandfather and Grandson by Patricia Espir (1997)

This grandad and grandson are walking in the park. Can you see any branches on the trees?

# The family on a picnic

Can you see the tiny dots that the artist has made his painting with?

19

# The family at the beach

Do you go to
the beach with
your family?

*Beach Scene* by Edgar Degas (c. 1876–77)

# The family at a party

This family are having a party by the river.

What do you think they are eating?

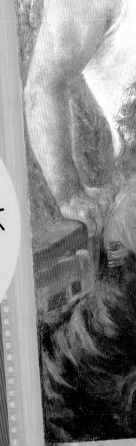

23

# Index

The end

## Notes for adults

This series covers the creative development area of learning. Each book looks at works of art from different cultures and different media. This set of books will support the young child's learning about the world around them and provide opportunities for them to explore different types of art. The following key Early Learning Goals are relevant to this series:
• explore colour, texture, shape, form and space in two or three dimensions
• respond in a variety of ways to what they see, hear, smell, touch and feel
• use their imagination in art and design.

**Lets Look at Families** includes the identification of different members of an extended family. Children are able to identify with their own family members and compare them. The book also explores the different techniques artists have used to represent different members of their own or others' families, using sculpture, paint and chalk.

Children will need to explore the differences between a 2-D painting and a 3-D sculpture and it will be necessary to explain that some artists represent their work in a literal way, like a photograph, while some paint or draw how an object 'feels' to them so it may not look like the 'real thing'. Discussing how some objects make children feel, or what they are reminded of when they see them, can help understanding.

Key vocabulary that can be explored through this book includes *photograph, painting, carved, stone, chalk, colours, marks, paintbrush, sculpture, pottery, light* and *dark*.

### Follow-up activities

Children could represent different family members in different ways. For example, mummy could be drawn with chalk, grandma painted, and sister drawn with pencils. These pictures could then be made into a book which represents each child's family and can be compared to show that all families are different. Parents could be warned so as to avoid sensitive situations, but also to encourage them to provide photographs, which could help the children.